MASTERING AUTONOMOUS

ROBOTICS WITH ROS2

AND PYTHON

A Hands-On Guide to Developing Intelligent Robot Behaviors for Navigation, Perception, and Autonomous Control

Wilson Hayes

Copyright © 2025 by Wilson Hayes

Table of Contents

Introduction

The Power of ROS2 and Python in Robotics

In today's rapidly evolving technological landscape, robotics is no longer a concept confined to research labs or high-tech manufacturing plants. Instead, it is becoming an integral part of everyday life, revolutionizing industries, enhancing human productivity, and even entering our homes. From autonomous delivery robots navigating busy city streets to robotic arms assembling products in factories with precision, the influence of robotics is growing at an unprecedented rate.

At the core of this transformation lies **ROS2 (Robot Operating System 2) and Python**—a powerful combination that enables developers, engineers, and hobbyists to build intelligent robots capable of sensing, reasoning, and acting autonomously in complex environments.

- **ROS2** provides a robust framework for designing modular and scalable robot applications. It enables seamless communication between robotic components, simplifies multi-robot collaboration, and enhances real-time performance, making it the preferred platform for cutting-edge robotics development.

- **Python**, with its simple yet powerful syntax, is the ideal programming language for robotics. Its vast ecosystem of libraries—including NumPy for numerical computation, OpenCV for computer vision, and TensorFlow for machine learning—allows developers to write efficient and flexible robotics applications.

By **combining ROS2 and Python**, this book empowers you to build autonomous robots from the ground up, enabling them to **perceive their surroundings, navigate through environments, manipulate objects, and interact with humans naturally**. Whether you are a complete beginner eager to step into the world of robotics or an experienced developer looking to enhance your skills, this book will guide you through every essential concept with **clear explanations, hands-on projects, and real-world examples**.

What You'll Gain from This Book

This book is **more than just a theoretical guide**—it's a hands-on learning journey. Each chapter is designed to **gradually build your robotics expertise**, starting from the foundational concepts and progressing to advanced topics.

Here's what you can expect:

1. **Understanding ROS2** – You'll learn the core concepts of ROS2, including nodes, topics, services, and actions, and how they enable seamless robot communication.

2. **Mastering Python for Robotics** – We'll cover the essential Python skills needed to write robotic applications, from basic programming concepts to advanced data processing techniques.

3. **Exploring Robot Perception** – You'll learn how robots interpret their surroundings using sensors like LiDAR, cameras, and ultrasonic detectors.

4. **Building Autonomous Navigation Systems** – We'll dive into motion planning, odometry, mapping, and real-time decision-making.

5. **Manipulating Objects and Interacting with Humans** – We'll explore robotic arms, grasping techniques, voice recognition, and human-robot interaction.

6. **Simulating Robots Before Deployment** – You'll discover how to use Gazebo and RViz to create and test robot models in virtual environments before deploying them in the real world.

7. **Debugging and Troubleshooting** – Robotics development comes with challenges. We'll provide strategies for debugging hardware, software, and network issues.

8. **The Future of Robotics** – We'll explore how AI, machine learning, and cloud robotics are shaping the next generation of intelligent robots.

Each chapter includes **hands-on projects, step-by-step tutorials, and code examples**, ensuring that you don't just read about robotics—you build, experiment, and apply your knowledge.

Who Should Read This Guide: Beginners, Hobbyists, and Professionals

This book is tailored for a diverse audience, making it **accessible to beginners** while also providing **valuable insights for experienced developers and researchers**.

- **Beginners and Students:** If you are new to robotics and have little to no experience with ROS2 or Python, this book will provide a structured learning path. You'll start with the basics and gradually progress to more complex projects, ensuring a smooth learning curve.

- **Hobbyists and DIY Enthusiasts:** If you enjoy building robots as a passion project, this book will introduce you to the latest tools and technologies, enabling you to create smarter, more capable robots.

- **Engineers and Professionals:** If you're a developer, researcher, or engineer working in robotics, this book will help you leverage ROS2's modular architecture and Python's powerful programming capabilities to build and optimize robotic systems efficiently.

Regardless of your background, by the time you complete this book, you'll be equipped with the skills to **develop intelligent robot behaviors, integrate multiple hardware components, and deploy fully autonomous robotic systems**.

How to Navigate This Book for Maximum Learning and Hands-On Practice

This book is designed for **progressive learning**, meaning each chapter builds upon the previous one. However, if you have prior experience in robotics, you can **jump to the chapters that interest you most**.

How to Get the Most Out of This Book

✅ **Follow the Hands-On Projects** – Each chapter includes practical projects that reinforce key concepts. Don't just read the code—**run it, modify it, experiment with it**.

✅ **Use Code Examples as a Learning Tool** – The book provides **fully documented Python scripts** for each project. You can use them as a foundation for your own robotics applications.

✓ **Leverage Diagrams and Illustrations** – Visualizing complex concepts is crucial. **Take your time to study the provided diagrams**, as they will help you understand robotic architectures more intuitively.

✓ **Explore Advanced Techniques** – Once you master the basics, dive into optimization techniques to improve performance, reliability, and real-time execution.

✓ **Troubleshoot Like a Pro** – Robotics development involves debugging. The troubleshooting sections will help you **diagnose and fix common errors**, ensuring smooth implementation.

The Expanding Role of Robotics in Modern Industries

Robotics is transforming nearly every industry, **enhancing efficiency, safety, and automation**. Some of the most exciting applications include:

- **Manufacturing & Industrial Automation:** Robotic arms assemble products with **unmatched speed and precision**, reducing production costs.

- **Healthcare & Medical Robotics:** Surgical robots assist doctors in performing delicate operations with **higher accuracy and minimal invasiveness**.

- **Autonomous Vehicles:** Self-driving cars use **robotic perception and AI-driven decision-making** to navigate roads safely.

- **Agriculture & Food Production:** Robots monitor crops, automate harvesting, and enhance food safety through **smart processing technologies**.

- **Space Exploration:** Autonomous rovers, such as NASA's Perseverance, explore **harsh extraterrestrial environments** with **intelligent navigation**.

With continued advancements in AI and machine learning, robots are becoming **more autonomous, adaptable, and intelligent**, paving the way for unprecedented innovations.

AI, Machine Learning, and the Future of Intelligent Robots

The next frontier in robotics lies at the intersection of **Artificial Intelligence (AI), Machine Learning (ML), and Cloud Computing**. These technologies are **enabling robots to learn from experience, adapt to new environments, and make autonomous decisions**.

- **AI-driven robots** can process massive amounts of sensor data in real time, improving their ability to **recognize objects, track movements, and interact naturally** with humans.

- **Machine learning algorithms** allow robots to continuously improve their **navigation, manipulation, and decision-making** capabilities based on real-world feedback.

- **Cloud robotics** is pushing collaboration to new heights—robots can now access **shared knowledge bases, receive over-the-air software updates, and process complex computations remotely**.

By the end of this book, you will not only understand how to **develop intelligent robotic systems** but also gain insight into the **exciting future of robotics, where AI-powered machines coexist with humans in a dynamic, automated world**.

Setting Up for Success: Tools, Resources, and Essential Software

Before diving into the hands-on projects, you'll need to **set up your development environment** with the following:

- **Operating System**: Ubuntu Linux (recommended), macOS, or Windows

- **ROS2**: The latest version, installed following step-by-step instructions

- **Python**: With essential libraries such as NumPy, OpenCV, and TensorFlow

- **Gazebo & RViz**: For robot simulation and visualization

- **Hardware**: (Optional) A Raspberry Pi, sensors, or robotic arms for real-world testing

Each chapter will guide you through **installing, configuring, and using these tools**, ensuring that you have a **fully functional robotics development environment**.

Final Thoughts

Robotics is one of the most exciting fields of the 21st century, and **this book is your gateway to mastering it**. By the time you reach the final chapter, you will have built **intelligent robotic behaviors from scratch**, empowering you to take on real-world challenges and **push the boundaries of innovation**.

Let's begin your robotics journey! 🚀

Chapter 1: ROS2 Fundamentals and Getting Started

Robotics is evolving at an unprecedented pace, and at the core of this revolution lies **ROS2 (Robot Operating System 2)**—a flexible, scalable, and high-performance framework designed for modern robotic applications. Whether you're building an autonomous vehicle, a robotic arm for industrial automation, or a drone for aerial navigation, **ROS2 provides the tools, libraries, and infrastructure** to bring your project to life efficiently.

ROS2 is more than just an upgrade from its predecessor, **ROS1**. It represents a **significant leap in robotic software engineering**, addressing the limitations of the original system while incorporating **real-time capabilities, multi-platform support, and enhanced security**. As the industry moves toward **autonomous, AI-driven robots**, ROS2 is setting the foundation for **next-generation robotic intelligence**.

What Makes ROS2 the Future of Robotics?

Robotics demands **high-performance computing, real-time processing, and robust communication** between hardware components. ROS2 is designed to meet these needs with:

- **Real-time capabilities** – Robots need to process sensor data and make decisions instantly. ROS2 introduces **real-time Quality of Service (QoS)** features, allowing systems to **prioritize critical tasks** with predictable execution.

- **Scalability and modularity** – Whether you're building a small robotic assistant or a large fleet of autonomous vehicles, ROS2 supports distributed systems, **allowing robots to communicate across networks seamlessly**.

- **Cross-platform compatibility** – Unlike ROS1, which was primarily Linux-based, ROS2 runs on **Linux, macOS, Windows, and embedded systems**, expanding its reach to more devices.

- **Enhanced security and stability** – ROS2 is built with **enterprise-grade security features**, making it a reliable choice for **mission-critical applications** in industries like healthcare, aerospace, and defense.

Key Differences Between ROS1 and ROS2

Feature	ROS1	ROS2
Real-Time Support	Limited	Full real-time support with DDS middleware
Multi-Platform Support	Linux only	Linux, macOS, Windows, and RTOS
Security Features	Minimal	Improved authentication and encryption
Scalability	Suitable for single robots	Designed for multi-robot and cloud-based deployments
Communication	Custom TCP-based messaging	Uses **DDS (Data Distribution Service)** for improved performance

The Evolution of Open-Source Robotics Frameworks

The need for a **flexible, open-source framework** led to the creation of ROS1 in 2007. However, as robots became **more complex and widespread**, the limitations of ROS1 became apparent. Industry leaders, including **Open Robotics, NASA, Intel, and Bosch**, collaborated to develop **ROS2**, incorporating modern software engineering best practices.

Today, ROS2 powers **autonomous drones, warehouse robots, medical assistants, and even space exploration systems**.

Essential ROS2 Concepts and Terminology

Before diving into hands-on projects, it's crucial to understand **ROS2's core concepts**.

Nodes, Topics, Messages, and Services

1. **Nodes** – The fundamental unit of ROS2 applications, representing **a single process executing a specific function** (e.g., reading sensor data, controlling motors).

2. **Topics** – Channels for **publish-subscribe communication** between nodes. A **sensor node** can

publish data on a topic, while multiple **subscriber nodes** receive and process the information.

3. **Messages** – The **data structure exchanged** over topics (e.g., sensor readings, velocity commands).

4. **Services** – Unlike topics, services use a **request-response model**, where a node sends a request, and another node processes and returns a response.

ROS2 Parameters and Packages Explained

- **Parameters** – Configurable values that allow **dynamic tuning** of node behavior without modifying code.

- **Packages** – ROS2 software modules containing **nodes, launch files, configuration files, and dependencies**, facilitating organized development.

Real-World Applications of ROS2

ROS2 is the backbone of **many cutting-edge robotic applications**.

Self-Driving Cars and Autonomous Navigation

Companies like **Tesla, Waymo, and Uber** rely on ROS2 for autonomous vehicle development, using its **real-time data handling and sensor fusion capabilities** for safe navigation.

Industrial and Manufacturing Robotics

Factories worldwide use **ROS2-powered robotic arms and autonomous mobile robots (AMRs)** for automated assembly lines, warehouse logistics, and **precision manufacturing**.

Aerial Drones and Last-Mile Delivery Bots

Companies like **Amazon Prime Air and Zipline** use ROS2 to control drones, ensuring **stable flight, accurate navigation, and object avoidance**.

Healthcare and Assistive Robotics

Surgical robots like **da Vinci** and rehabilitation exoskeletons use **ROS2 for precise movement and adaptive control**, assisting in **delicate surgeries and patient mobility**.

AI in Space Exploration and Research

NASA uses ROS2 in **Mars rovers and space robotic systems**, leveraging **AI-driven decision-making** and robust communication in extreme environments.

Setting Up the ROS2 Development Environment

To start developing with ROS2, we need to **install and configure the necessary tools**.

Installing ROS2 on Ubuntu Linux

1. **Update system packages**:

bash

CopyEdit

sudo apt update && sudo apt upgrade -y

2. **Install ROS2 dependencies**:

bash

CopyEdit

sudo apt install curl gnupg lsb-release

3. **Add the ROS2 repository** and install:

bash

CopyEdit

sudo apt install ros-humble-desktop

Alternative Setup for macOS and Windows Users

For macOS:

- Install ROS2 via **Homebrew and Docker** For Windows:

- Use **WSL (Windows Subsystem for Linux) + Ubuntu**

Understanding the ROS2 File System and Workspace Organization

A **ROS2 workspace** contains:

- **src/** – Source code (nodes, packages)

- **install/** – Compiled executables

- **build/** – Intermediate files

- **log/** – System logs

Building Your First ROS2 Project

Let's **create and run our first ROS2 application**.

Creating and Managing ROS2 Packages

    1. Create a workspace:

bash

CopyEdit

```
mkdir -p ~/ros2_ws/src

cd ~/ros2_ws
```

    2. Create a package:

bash

CopyEdit

```
ros2 pkg create my_robot --build-type ament_python
```

Writing Your First Publisher and Subscriber Node in Python

Publisher (talker.py):

python

CopyEdit

```python
import rclpy

from rclpy.node import Node

from std_msgs.msg import String


class Talker(Node):

    def __init__(self):

        super().__init__('talker')

        self.publisher_ = self.create_publisher(String, 'chatter', 10)

        self.timer = self.create_timer(1, self.publish_message)


    def publish_message(self):

        msg = String()

        msg.data = "Hello from ROS2!"

        self.publisher_.publish(msg)

        self.get_logger().info(f'Publishing: {msg.data}')
```

```
rclpy.init()

node = Talker()

rclpy.spin(node)

node.destroy_node()

rclpy.shutdown()
```

Run with:

bash

CopyEdit

```
ros2 run my_robot talker
```

Running and Debugging ROS2 Nodes

To list running nodes:

bash

CopyEdit

```
ros2 node list
```

Advanced ROS2 Optimization and Best Practices

Quality of Service (QoS) in ROS2 Communication

QoS settings **prioritize critical messages**, ensuring real-time execution in robots.

Automating Processes with ROS2 Launch Files

Launch multiple nodes automatically:

xml

CopyEdit

```xml
<launch>
  <node name="talker" pkg="my_robot" exec="talker.py"/>
  <node name="listener" pkg="my_robot" exec="listener.py"/>
</launch>
```

ROS2 Bag Files for Data Logging and Analysis

Record sensor data:

bash

CopyEdit

```
ros2 bag record -a
```

Troubleshooting Common Issues in ROS2 Development

1. **Debugging "Package Not Found" Errors**

   o Run colcon build and source install/setup.bash

2. **Resolving Topic and Service Communication Failures**

   o Check ros2 topic list for available topics

3. **Fixing Message Type Mismatches and Build Errors**

   o Ensure correct message types using ros2 interface show <message_type>

Key Takeaways and Next Steps in ROS2 Mastery

- ROS2 **enhances robotic autonomy, communication, and real-time processing**.

- It powers **self-driving cars, industrial robots, drones, and space exploration**.

- Hands-on experience with **nodes, topics, QoS, and debugging** is crucial.

Chapter 2: Python for Robotics – A Practical Approach

Python has become the **go-to programming language for robotics development**, particularly when working with **ROS2 (Robot Operating System 2)**. With its **readable syntax, powerful libraries, and vast community support**, Python enables **rapid prototyping, efficient data handling, and AI-driven automation** in robotics.

In this chapter, we will explore **why Python is the best language for robotics, essential concepts for ROS2 development, setting up a Python development environment, hands-on ROS2 projects, and advanced debugging techniques**. By the end, you will have the skills to **write, test, and optimize Python code for ROS2-powered robots**.

Why Python is the Best Language for Robotics

Python's dominance in robotics is driven by its:

1. **Ease of Learning and Readability** – Python's syntax is **intuitive**, making it ideal for beginners and professionals alike.

2. **Rich Ecosystem of Libraries** – Libraries like **NumPy, OpenCV, SciPy, and TensorFlow** simplify **sensor data processing, AI integration, and motion planning**.

3. **Seamless Integration with ROS2** – Python's **rclpy package** allows developers to write **ROS2 nodes**, manage robotic behaviors, and **communicate efficiently** with sensors and actuators.

4. **Rapid Prototyping and Testing** – Python accelerates **algorithm development**, allowing **real-time testing** without extensive compilation processes.

5. **Cross-Platform Support** – Python runs on **Linux, Windows, macOS, and embedded systems**, making it highly flexible.

In ROS2-based robotics, Python is used for:

- **Writing ROS2 nodes (talkers, listeners, service handlers)**

- **Controlling robot actuators and motors**

- **Processing sensor data from LiDAR, cameras, and IMUs**

- **Implementing AI-driven decision-making**

Essential Python Concepts for ROS2 Development

Before writing ROS2 applications in Python, you must understand **core programming concepts** that are essential for robotics.

Data Structures and Algorithmic Thinking

Robots rely on **efficient data structures and algorithms** for processing information and making decisions. Some key data structures include:

- **Lists** – Used for **storing sensor data**, waypoints, and movement commands.

- **Dictionaries** – Essential for **storing key-value pairs**, such as mapping sensor IDs to their data values.

- **Tuples** – Useful for representing **fixed coordinate points or RGB color values**.

- **Queues and Stacks** – Applied in **task scheduling, depth-first search (DFS), and breadth-first search (BFS) algorithms** for robotic path planning.

Example: Storing LiDAR sensor readings in a Python list:

python

CopyEdit

```python
lidar_data = [0.5, 0.8, 1.2, 0.7, 0.6]  # Distances from obstacles in meters

print(f"Closest obstacle detected at {min(lidar_data)} meters")
```

Object-Oriented Programming for Robotics

Python's **Object-Oriented Programming (OOP)** model helps in designing **modular, reusable, and scalable robotics applications**.

- **Classes and Objects** – Define robot behaviors and attributes in a structured manner.

- **Encapsulation** – Protects data and prevents unintended modifications.

- **Inheritance** – Enables code reuse across different robot types.

- **Polymorphism** – Simplifies controlling multiple robot components with a single interface.

Example: A simple class for a mobile robot:

python

CopyEdit

```
class Robot:
    def __init__(self, name, speed):
        self.name = name
```

```python
        self.speed = speed


    def move(self):

        print(f"{self.name} is moving at {self.speed} m/s")


robot1 = Robot("ExplorerBot", 1.5)

robot1.move()
```

Using Python Libraries: NumPy, OpenCV, SciPy, and More

Python's extensive libraries simplify complex robotics tasks.

NumPy – Efficient Numerical Computations

- Used for **matrix operations, sensor data filtering, and kinematics calculations**.

- Example: Converting LiDAR data into a NumPy array for analysis:

python

CopyEdit

```python
import numpy as np

lidar_readings = np.array([0.5, 0.8, 1.2, 0.7, 0.6])

print(f"Mean distance to obstacles: {np.mean(lidar_readings)} meters")
```

OpenCV – Computer Vision and Image Processing

- Applied in **object detection, edge detection, and SLAM (Simultaneous Localization and Mapping)**.

- Example: Loading and displaying an image from a robot's camera:

python

CopyEdit

```python
import cv2

image = cv2.imread("robot_view.jpg")

cv2.imshow("Robot Camera", image)

cv2.waitKey(0)

cv2.destroyAllWindows()
```

SciPy – Advanced Scientific Computations

- Used in **optimization, signal processing, and physics-based simulations**.

- Example: Applying a Gaussian filter to smooth noisy sensor readings:

python

CopyEdit

```
from scipy.ndimage import gaussian_filter

smoothed_data = gaussian_filter(lidar_readings, sigma=1)

print(smoothed_data)
```

Setting Up a Python Development Environment for ROS2

Before writing Python-based ROS2 applications, set up the **development environment**.

1. **Install Python 3 and Pip**

bash

CopyEdit

sudo apt update

sudo apt install python3 python3 pip

2. **Set Up a Virtual Environment for ROS2 Projects**

bash

CopyEdit

python3 -m venv ros2_env

source ros2_env/bin/activate

3. **Install ROS2 Python Packages**

bash

CopyEdit

```bash
pip install rclpy numpy opencv-python scipy
```

Hands-on Python Projects in ROS2

Simulating and Controlling Robot Movements in Gazebo

Gazebo is a **powerful physics simulator** for testing robots in a virtual environment.

1. **Launch a Gazebo simulation:**

bash

CopyEdit

```
ros2 launch gazebo_ros gazebo.launch.py
```

2. **Write a Python script to move the robot:**

python

CopyEdit

```python
import rclpy
from geometry_msgs.msg import Twist
```

```python
from rclpy.node import Node

class MoveRobot(Node):
    def __init__(self):
        super().__init__('move_robot')
        self.publisher = self.create_publisher(Twist, '/cmd_vel', 10)
        self.timer = self.create_timer(1.0, self.move)

    def move(self):
        msg = Twist()
        msg.linear.x = 0.5  # Move forward
        self.publisher.publish(msg)
        self.get_logger().info("Robot moving forward")

rclpy.init()
node = MoveRobot()
```

```
rclpy.spin(node)
```

Implementing Sensor-Based Obstacle Avoidance

Using **LiDAR or ultrasonic sensors**, we can create an **obstacle avoidance algorithm**.

python

CopyEdit

```python
import rclpy

from sensor_msgs.msg import LaserScan

from geometry_msgs.msg import Twist


class ObstacleAvoidance:

    def __init__(self, node):

        self.node = node

        self.publisher = node.create_publisher(Twist, '/cmd_vel', 10)
```

```python
        node.create_subscription(LaserScan,                '/scan',
self.process_scan, 10)


    def process_scan(self, msg):

        min_distance = min(msg.ranges)

        cmd = Twist()

        if min_distance < 0.5:

            cmd.angular.z = 0.5  # Turn

        else:

            cmd.linear.x = 0.5  # Move forward

        self.publisher.publish(cmd)


rclpy.init()

node = rclpy.create_node('obstacle_avoidance')

ObstacleAvoidance(node)

rclpy.spin(node)
```

Advanced Python Techniques for Robotics Programming

1. **Multithreading for Parallel Processing**

python

CopyEdit

```python
import threading

def sensor_data():
    while True:
        print("Processing sensor data...")


thread = threading.Thread(target=sensor_data)

thread.start()
```

2. **Machine Learning for Robot Decision-Making**

   o Use **Scikit-Learn or TensorFlow** to train a robot to **recognize obstacles and respond intelligently**.

Debugging with ROS2 Logging

python

CopyEdit

```
self.get_logger().info("Obstacle detected, turning right")
```

1. **Profiling Code for Performance Bottlenecks**

python

CopyEdit

```
import cProfile

cProfile.run('my_function()')
```

2. **Memory Optimization with Generators**

python

CopyEdit

```
def sensor_readings():
    while True:
        yield get_sensor_data()
```

Conclusion

- **Python is the backbone of ROS2-based robotics** due to its **simplicity, power, and vast ecosystem**.

- **Mastering Python libraries, OOP, and Gazebo simulations** is crucial for robotic software development.

- **Hands-on experience with Python projects** in ROS2 will enhance your robotics proficiency.

Chapter 3: Understanding Robotics Hardware and Simulation

Robotics is a **multidisciplinary field** that brings together **mechanical engineering, electronics, and software development** to create intelligent machines capable of performing complex tasks. To develop functional robots, it is crucial to understand the **hardware components** that drive their behavior and the **simulation tools** that allow us to test and refine their capabilities before real-world deployment.

This chapter provides an in-depth exploration of **robotic hardware**, including **sensors, actuators, and microcontrollers**, and their integration with **ROS2 (Robot Operating System 2)**. Additionally, we will delve into **robot simulation using Gazebo**, a powerful tool for testing robotic systems in virtual environments. Finally, we will engage in a **hands-on project to design and control a robot using ROS2**, providing a practical foundation for building real-world autonomous systems.

Fundamentals of Robotics Engineering

Robots are composed of several key components that enable them to **perceive their surroundings, process information, and take action**. These components include:

- **Sensors** – The robot's **eyes and ears**, used for detecting the environment.

- **Actuators** – The **muscles** that move the robot.

- **Microcontrollers and Embedded Systems** – The **brain** that processes data and makes decisions.

- **ROS2 Framework** – The **nervous system** that facilitates communication between hardware and software.

How Sensors, Actuators, and Microcontrollers Work

Sensors: Enabling Robot Perception

Sensors allow robots to **detect, analyze, and interact** with their environment. Common types of sensors include:

Sensor Type	Function	Common Uses in Robotics

LiDAR (Light Detection and Ranging)	Measures distance using laser beams	Mapping, obstacle avoidance, SLAM
Ultrasonic Sensors	Uses sound waves to detect objects	Proximity sensing, collision avoidance
Cameras	Captures visual data for processing	Object recognition, navigation, vision-based control
IMU (Inertial Measurement Unit)	Measures acceleration, rotation, and orientation	Motion tracking, stabilization, self-balancing robots
Temperature Sensors	Detects heat and temperature variations	Environmental monitoring, safety applications

Example: Using a LiDAR Sensor with ROS2

python

CopyEdit

```python
import rclpy

from sensor_msgs.msg import LaserScan


def lidar_callback(msg):
    min_distance = min(msg.ranges)
    print(f"Closest object detected at {min_distance} meters")


rclpy.init()
node = rclpy.create_node("lidar_listener")
node.create_subscription(LaserScan, "/scan", lidar_callback, 10)
rclpy.spin(node)
```

Actuators: The Muscles of a Robot

Actuators convert electrical signals into mechanical movement. Common actuators include:

- **DC Motors** – Used for wheels, arms, and rotating components.

- **Servo Motors** – Used for precise movements, such as robotic arms.

- **Stepper Motors** – Used for precise, incremental motion control.

- **Hydraulic and Pneumatic Actuators** – Used in heavy-duty robotic applications.

Example: Controlling a Robot's Motion with ROS2

python

CopyEdit

```
import rclpy

from geometry_msgs.msg import Twist


def move_robot():
    rclpy.init()
    node = rclpy.create_node("robot_mover")
    pub = node.create_publisher(Twist, "/cmd_vel", 10)
```

```
move_cmd = Twist()

move_cmd.linear.x = 0.5  # Move forward

pub.publish(move_cmd)

node.get_logger().info("Robot is moving forward!")


rclpy.spin(node)


move_robot()
```

Microcontrollers: The Brain of the Robot

Microcontrollers process sensor data and send commands to actuators. **Popular microcontrollers used in robotics include:**

- **Arduino** – Great for beginners and small robotic projects.

- **Raspberry Pi** – More powerful, supports AI-based applications.

- **NVIDIA Jetson** – Used for AI and deep learning robotics applications.

Microcontrollers interact with **ROS2 via serial communication** using protocols like **I2C, SPI, or UART**.

The Role of ROS2 in Coordinating Robot Behavior

ROS2 is the **software backbone of modern robotics**, enabling seamless communication between different components. It provides:

- **Nodes** – Independent programs that handle different robotic tasks.

- **Topics** – Message-passing channels between nodes.

- **Services** – Request-response interactions between components.

- **Actions** – Enables long-running processes, like navigation.

Example: ROS2 Communication Between a Sensor Node and a Motor Node

1. **Sensor Node (publishes distance data):**

python

CopyEdit

```
import rclpy
from std_msgs.msg import Float32


node = rclpy.create_node("sensor_node")
pub = node.create_publisher(Float32, "/distance", 10)


msg = Float32()
msg.data = 1.5  # Simulated distance data
pub.publish(msg)
```

2. Motor Node (subscribes to distance data and moves accordingly):

python

CopyEdit

```python
import rclpy

from std_msgs.msg import Float32

from geometry_msgs.msg import Twist


def callback(msg):
    move_cmd = Twist()
    if msg.data < 0.5:
        move_cmd.linear.x = 0.0  # Stop if an obstacle is too close
    else:
        move_cmd.linear.x = 0.5  # Move forward
    pub.publish(move_cmd)


rclpy.init()
```

```
node = rclpy.create_node("motor_controller")

pub = node.create_publisher(Twist, "/cmd_vel", 10)

node.create_subscription(Float32, "/distance", callback, 10)

rclpy.spin(node)
```

Simulating Robots in Gazebo

Gazebo is a **3D physics-based simulator** that allows developers to test robots **without physical hardware.**

Setting Up a Virtual Robot Environment

1. **Install Gazebo with ROS2**

bash

CopyEdit

```
sudo apt install ros-foxy-gazebo-ros-pkgs
```

2. **Launch a Gazebo Simulation**

bash

CopyEdit

```
ros2 launch gazebo_ros gazebo.launch.py
```

3. **Spawn a Robot Model in Gazebo**

bash

CopyEdit

```
ros2 run gazebo_ros spawn_entity.py -file my_robot.urdf -entity my_robot
```

Running and Testing Robot Models in Simulation

Gazebo allows developers to:

- **Test motion algorithms** before real-world deployment.
- **Simulate sensor behavior** (camera, LiDAR, IMU).
- **Refine robot design** using **URDF (Unified Robot Description Format)** files.

Example: URDF File for a Simple Wheeled Robot

xml

CopyEdit

```xml
<robot name="simple_robot">
```

```
<link name="base_link">

  <visual>

   <geometry>

    <box size="0.5 0.3 0.2"/>

   </geometry>

   <material name="blue"/>

  </visual>

 </link>

</robot>
```

Loading the Model in Gazebo

bash

CopyEdit

```
ros2 launch gazebo_ros empty_world.launch.py

ros2 run gazebo_ros spawn_entity.py -file simple_robot.urdf -entity my_robot
```

Hands-on Project: Designing and Controlling a Robot in ROS2

Step 1: Define the Robot Model (URDF)

- Create a **wheeled robot model** using a **URDF file**.

- Add **sensors and actuators**.

Step 2: Implement ROS2 Nodes for Movement

- Write a **ROS2 node to control motion using a joystick or keyboard**.

Step 3: Simulate the Robot In Gazebo

- Load the **URDF file into Gazebo**.

- Test **sensor integration and obstacle avoidance**.

Step 4: Visualize Data in RViz

- Use **RViz** to monitor **sensor feedback and movement commands**.

bash

CopyEdit

```
ros2 launch rviz2 rviz2.launch.py
```

Chapter 4: Robot Perception and Sensor Fusion

In the world of autonomous robotics, **perception** is the key to intelligent decision-making. Robots must be able to **see, sense, and interpret** their surroundings to navigate safely and complete tasks effectively. **Sensor fusion**, the process of combining multiple sensor inputs, allows robots to develop a more **accurate, robust, and reliable** understanding of their environment.

In this chapter, we'll explore:

- **Different types of sensors** used in robotics, such as LiDAR, depth cameras, and proximity sensors.

- **How to process and analyze sensor data** using ROS2 and Python.

- **A hands-on project: Building a computer vision-based line-following robot**.

- **Advanced sensor integration techniques** to enhance robot perception.

By the end of this chapter, you will have a strong understanding of **how to integrate and optimize sensors** in ROS2-powered robotic systems.

Types of Sensors Used in Autonomous Robots

Autonomous robots rely on various **sensors** to collect information about their environment. Below are some of the most commonly used sensors in robotics and their functions.

Sensor Type	Function	Common Applications
LiDAR (Light Detection and Ranging)	Uses laser beams to measure distances and generate a 3D map of the environment	Obstacle detection, SLAM (Simultaneous Localization and Mapping), autonomous vehicles
Proximity Sensors	Detects objects within a certain range using infrared, ultrasonic, or	Collision avoidance, object detection

	capacitive technology	
Depth Cameras (RGB-D Sensors)	Captures depth information along with RGB images for 3D perception	Object recognition, autonomous grasping, terrain mapping
IMU (Inertial Measurement Unit)	Measures acceleration and angular velocity for motion tracking	Navigation, stability control
GPS (Global Positioning System)	Provides absolute position data using satellite signals	Outdoor navigation, UAVs, agricultural robotics

LiDAR: Mapping the World with Laser Precision

LiDAR sensors work by emitting **laser pulses** and measuring the time it takes for the light to reflect off surfaces and return to the sensor. This information is used to **create a detailed 3D representation** of the robot's surroundings.

Example: Publishing LiDAR Data in ROS2

```python
CopyEdit
import rclpy
from sensor_msgs.msg import LaserScan

def lidar_callback(msg):
    print(f"Closest object detected at {min(msg.ranges)} meters")

rclpy.init()
node = rclpy.create_node("lidar_listener")
node.create_subscription(LaserScan, "/scan", lidar_callback, 10)
rclpy.spin(node)
```

Processing and Analyzing Sensor Data in ROS2 and Python

Once a robot collects data from sensors, it must **process, analyze, and make decisions** based on that data. In ROS2, sensor data is typically processed using **topics and messages**.

Subscribing to Sensor Topics in ROS2

Each sensor **publishes data** to a topic, and **subscriber nodes** process that data.

Example: Reading Camera Data in ROS2

python

CopyEdit

```
import rclpy

from sensor_msgs.msg import Image

from cv_bridge import CvBridge

import cv2


def image_callback(msg):
```

```
bridge = CvBridge()

frame = bridge.imgmsg_to_cv2(msg, "bgr8")

cv2.imshow("Robot Camera View", frame)

cv2.waitKey(1)


rclpy.init()

node = rclpy.create_node("camera_listener")

node.create_subscription(Image,        "/camera/image_raw",
image_callback, 10)

rclpy.spin(node)
```

Sensor Fusion: Combining Multiple Inputs

Sensor fusion helps **reduce noise and improve accuracy** by integrating data from different sensors.

- **Example 1:** Combining LiDAR and Camera data for **better obstacle detection**.

- **Example 2:** Merging IMU and GPS data to **enhance localization accuracy**.

Example: Combining IMU and GPS Data

```python
CopyEdit
import rclpy
from sensor_msgs.msg import NavSatFix, Imu


def gps_callback(msg):
    print(f"GPS Coordinates: {msg.latitude}, {msg.longitude}")


def imu_callback(msg):
    print(f"IMU Orientation: {msg.orientation}")


rclpy.init()
node = rclpy.create_node("sensor_fusion_node")
node.create_subscription(NavSatFix, "/gps/fix", gps_callback, 10)
node.create_subscription(Imu, "/imu/data", imu_callback, 10)
```

```
rclpy.spin(node)
```

Building a Computer Vision-Based Line-Following Robot

A **line-following robot** is a common robotics project where a robot detects and follows a **predefined path** using **computer vision and image processing techniques**.

Project Overview

Goal: Build a robot that can follow a black line on a white surface using a **camera and OpenCV**.

Step 1: Setting Up the Camera in ROS2

Ensure the camera is properly connected and publishing data to a ROS2 topic:

bash

CopyEdit

```
ros2 topic list
```

You should see something like /camera/image_raw.

Step 2: Writing the Image Processing Code

We will use **OpenCV** to detect the black line and send movement commands to the robot.

python

CopyEdit

```python
import rclpy

from sensor_msgs.msg import Image

from cv_bridge import CvBridge

import cv2

import numpy as np

from geometry_msgs.msg import Twist


def process_image(msg):

    bridge = CvBridge()

    frame = bridge.imgmsg_to_cv2(msg, "bgr8")
```

```python
gray = cv2.cvtColor(frame, cv2.COLOR_BGR2GRAY)

_, threshold = cv2.threshold(gray, 120, 255, cv2.THRESH_BINARY_INV)


M = cv2.moments(threshold)
if M["m00"] != 0:
    cx = int(M["m10"] / M["m00"])
    error = cx - (frame.shape[1] // 2)


    twist = Twist()
    twist.linear.x = 0.2
    twist.angular.z = -error / 100
    pub.publish(twist)


cv2.imshow("Processed Image", threshold)
cv2.waitKey(1)
```

```
rclpy.init()

node = rclpy.create_node("line_follower")

pub = node.create_publisher(Twist, "/cmd_vel", 10)

node.create_subscription(Image,        "/camera/image_raw",
process_image, 10)

rclpy.spin(node)
```

Advanced Sensor Integration for Enhanced Robot Awareness

1. Multi-Sensor Fusion for Autonomous Navigation

Robots use **multiple sensors simultaneously** to **improve navigation accuracy**.

Example **Sensor Fusion Strategies**:

- **IMU + GPS for outdoor navigation.**

- **LiDAR + Depth Camera for obstacle detection.**

- **Proximity Sensors + Ultrasonic for precise positioning.**

Example: Fusing LiDAR and Ultrasonic Data

python

CopyEdit

```python
import rclpy

from sensor_msgs.msg import LaserScan, Range


def lidar_callback(msg):
    print(f"LiDAR detected obstacle at {min(msg.ranges)} meters")


def ultrasonic_callback(msg):
    print(f"Ultrasonic sensor detected object at {msg.range} meters")


rclpy.init()
node = rclpy.create_node("fusion_node")
```

```
node.create_subscription(LaserScan, "/scan", lidar_callback,
10)

node.create_subscription(Range,                "/ultrasonic",
ultrasonic_callback, 10)

rclpy.spin(node)
```

2. Improving Perception with AI and Deep Learning

- **AI-powered Object Recognition**

- **Deep Learning for Gesture Recognition**

- **Neural Networks for Autonomous Decision-Making**

Example: **Using a Pre-Trained AI Model for Object Recognition**

python

CopyEdit

```
import cv2

import torch

from torchvision import models, transforms
```

```python
model = models.resnet18(pretrained=True)

model.eval()


def recognize_object(image):

    preprocess = transforms.Compose([

        transforms.Resize(256),

        transforms.CenterCrop(224),

        transforms.ToTensor()

    ])

    img_tensor = preprocess(image).unsqueeze(0)

    output = model(img_tensor)

    print(f"Detected Object: {torch.argmax(output)}")
```

Chapter 5: Robot Navigation and Path Planning

Navigation is one of the most **critical capabilities** of autonomous robots. Whether it's a self-driving car navigating city streets, a warehouse robot transporting goods, or a drone mapping a disaster zone, a robot must **understand its surroundings, plan efficient paths, and dynamically adjust** to obstacles.

In this chapter, we will explore:

- The **fundamentals of robot motion and mapping**.

- How robots use **odometry, localization, and coordinate systems** to understand their position.

- **Motion planning strategies** for efficient navigation.

- Hands-on navigation projects, including implementing the **ROS2 Navigation Stack** and programming a robot to navigate a **maze**.

- Advanced topics such as **multi-robot coordination, real-time obstacle avoidance, and adaptive path planning**.

- Common **debugging strategies** to enhance navigation accuracy.

By the end of this chapter, you will have a **solid foundation in robot navigation** and practical experience implementing **path planning algorithms** in **ROS2**.

Understanding Robot Motion and Mapping

A robot must have a clear **understanding of its environment and position** before it can navigate effectively. This is achieved through a combination of **coordinate systems, odometry, and localization techniques**.

1. Coordinate Systems in Robotics

Robots operate within a **defined coordinate system** that helps them **position themselves relative to objects and the environment**.

- **Global Coordinate System (World Frame)**: A fixed reference frame in which all positions are measured.

- **Local Coordinate System (Robot Frame)**: A frame centered on the robot, where movements are defined relative to its own position.

In ROS2, **TF (Transform Library)** is used to manage **coordinate transformations** between different frames.

Example: Viewing TF Frames in ROS2

bash

CopyEdit

ros2 run tf2_tools view_frames.py

2. Odometry: Measuring Robot Motion

Odometry is the process of estimating a robot's position based on **wheel encoder data**. However, odometry alone is **prone to drift** over time.

Key Concepts in Odometry:

- **Linear and Angular Velocity**: Tracks forward/backward and rotational movement.

- **Encoder Readings**: Measure wheel rotations to estimate displacement.

- **Dead Reckoning**: Predicts the robot's future position based on past movements.

Example: Publishing Odometry Data in ROS2

python

CopyEdit

```python
import rclpy

from nav_msgs.msg import Odometry


def odometry_callback(msg):
    print(f"Robot Position: x={msg.pose.pose.position.x}, y={msg.pose.pose.position.y}")


rclpy.init()

node = rclpy.create_node("odometry_listener")

node.create_subscription(Odometry, "/odom", odometry_callback, 10)
```

rclpy.spin(node)

3. Localization: Understanding Position in a Dynamic World

Since odometry **accumulates errors over time**, robots use **localization algorithms** to maintain accurate positioning.

Common Localization Methods:

- **AMCL (Adaptive Monte Carlo Localization)**: Uses a **particle filter** to estimate robot position.

- **SLAM (Simultaneous Localization and Mapping)**: Builds a **map of the environment** while localizing the robot within it.

Example: Running AMCL Localization in ROS2

bash

CopyEdit

```
ros2 launch nav2_bringup localization_launch.py map:=your_map.yaml
```

Motion Planning Strategies for Mobile Robots

Motion planning allows robots to compute an **efficient, collision-free path** to a goal location.

1. Global vs. Local Path Planning

- **Global Path Planning**: Generates an overall path **from start to destination** (e.g., A* Algorithm, Dijkstra's Algorithm).

- **Local Path Planning**: Adjusts the robot's movement dynamically to **avoid obstacles** (e.g., Dynamic Window Approach, TEB Planner).

2. Common Path Planning Algorithms

Algorithm	Type	Use Case
A*	Global	Grid-based pathfinding for structured environments
Dijkstra's Algorithm	Global	Finds the shortest path without considering efficiency
RRT (Rapidly-exploring Random Trees)	Global	Effective for high-dimensional, complex spaces

DWA (Dynamic Window Approach)	Local	Used for real-time obstacle avoidance
TEB (Timed Elastic Band)	Local	Optimizes paths dynamically for smooth navigation

Hands-on Navigation Projects in ROS2

1. Implementing the ROS2 Navigation Stack

The **ROS2 Navigation Stack (Nav2)** is a collection of packages that handle robot navigation.

Step 1: Installing and Setting Up Nav2

bash

CopyEdit

sudo apt install ros-foxy-navigation2 ros-foxy-nav2-bringup

Step 2: Launching the Navigation Stack

bash

CopyEdit

```bash
ros2 launch nav2_bringup navigation_launch.py
```

Step 3: Sending a Goal to the Robot

bash

CopyEdit

```
ros2 action send_goal /navigate_to_pose
nav2_msgs/action/NavigateToPose "{pose: {position: {x: 2.0,
y: 3.0, z: 0.0}}}"
```

2. Programming a Robot to Navigate a Maze

Step 1: Creating a Maze Environment in Gazebo

bash

CopyEdit

```
ros2 launch gazebo_ros empty_world.launch.py
```

Step 2: Implementing Wall-Following Logic in Python

python

CopyEdit

```python
import rclpy

from sensor_msgs.msg import LaserScan
```

```python
from geometry_msgs.msg import Twist

def lidar_callback(msg):
    twist = Twist()
    if min(msg.ranges) < 0.5:
        twist.angular.z = 0.5  # Turn to avoid collision
    else:
        twist.linear.x = 0.2  # Move forward
    pub.publish(twist)

rclpy.init()
node = rclpy.create_node("maze_navigator")
pub = node.create_publisher(Twist, "/cmd_vel", 10)
node.create_subscription(LaserScan, "/scan", lidar_callback, 10)
rclpy.spin(node)
```

Advanced Navigation Techniques

1. Multi-Robot Coordination and Swarm Robotics

When multiple robots operate in the same environment, they must **coordinate their movements** to avoid collisions and work efficiently.

Multi-Robot Planning Approaches:

- **Decentralized Planning**: Each robot makes independent decisions.

- **Centralized Planning**: A central controller coordinates multiple robots.

Example: Running Multiple Robots in ROS2

bash

CopyEdit

```
ros2 launch nav2_bringup multi_robot_navigation.launch.py
```

2. Real-Time Obstacle Avoidance and Adaptive Path Planning

Real-time navigation requires **continuous adaptation** to obstacles in dynamic environments.

- **Obstacle Detection Using LiDAR and Depth Cameras.**

- **Reactive Path Adjustments with the Dynamic Window Approach (DWA).**

Example: Implementing DWA for Dynamic Path Adjustment

bash

CopyEdit

ros2 param set /local_planner use_dwa true

Debugging Navigation Errors and Enhancing Accuracy

Even the best-planned navigation systems encounter errors. Below are some **common issues and fixes**.

Issue	Cause	Solution
Robot moves in circles	Incorrect TF transforms	Check ros2 run tf2_tools view_frames.py
Navigation stack crashes	Configuration errors	Review params.yaml settings
Robot stops unexpectedly	Sensor failure or safety timeout	Ensure sensors are publishing correct data
Localization drift	Odometry errors	Use **AMCL** or SLAM for correction

Chapter 6: Decision-Making and Behavior Trees

Robots are no longer simple machines that follow pre-programmed paths or execute repetitive tasks. In modern robotics, **decision-making** plays a crucial role in enabling robots to **adapt, respond, and interact intelligently** with their environment. Whether it's a self-driving car deciding when to change lanes, a robotic vacuum navigating obstacles, or an autonomous drone adjusting its route based on weather conditions, the ability to make decisions is fundamental to autonomy.

One of the most effective ways to structure decision-making in robotics is through **Behavior Trees (BTs)**. Originally developed for game AI, behavior trees have proven highly effective in robotics due to their **modular, flexible, and reusable** nature. In this chapter, we will explore:

- **How robots make decisions** using behavior trees.

- **Programming AI-based behavior trees in ROS2** for intelligent decision-making.

- **Developing a robot that detects and reacts to objects** in real time.

By the end of this chapter, you will understand how to structure complex robotic behaviors **hierarchically**, ensuring **scalability, modularity, and adaptability** in autonomous robots.

How Robots Make Decisions Using Behavior Trees

1. What Are Behavior Trees?

Behavior Trees (BTs) are a **graph-based decision-making model** that organizes robotic behaviors in a structured hierarchy. Unlike traditional **finite state machines (FSMs)**, behavior trees offer:

✓ **Modularity** – Behaviors are independent and reusable.

✓ **Scalability** – Large systems can be structured efficiently.

✓ **Flexibility** – Behaviors can adapt dynamically to changes in the environment.

✓ **Readability** – The hierarchical nature makes debugging easier.

2. Structure of a Behavior Tree

A behavior tree consists of **nodes**, each serving a specific role in decision-making.

Types of Nodes in Behavior Trees

Node Type	Function	Example
Root Node	The starting point of the decision process	Top-level behavior (e.g., "Patrol the Area")
Control Nodes	Directs execution of child nodes	Sequences, Selectors, and Decorators
Leaf Nodes	Perform actions or check conditions	"Move to Goal," "Check Object Detection"

1. **Sequence Node (→)**: Executes child nodes from left to right. If a child **fails**, the sequence **stops**.

2. **Selector Node (?)**: Runs children until **one succeeds**.

3. **Decorator Node (↻)**: Modifies child behavior (e.g., repeats actions, adds delays).

4. **Action Node (🏃)**: Executes a robot action (e.g., "Move Forward").

5. **Condition Node (✅)**: Checks a condition (e.g., "Is Object Detected?").

Example of a Simple Behavior Tree for Obstacle Avoidance

mathematica

CopyEdit

```
Root
|
|    ─ Sequence (→)
|    ├── Condition: "Obstacle Detected?" ✅
|    ├── Action: "Stop Movement" 🏃
|    ├── Action: "Turn Left" 🏃
|    ├── Action: "Move Forward" 🏃
|
└── Selector (?)
     ├── Action: "Continue Moving Forward" 🏃
```

├── Action: "Search for a New Path" 🏃

Programming AI-Based Behavior Trees in ROS2

ROS2 provides **BehaviorTree.CPP**, a powerful library for implementing behavior trees in robotic applications.

1. Installing BehaviorTree.CPP in ROS2

bash

CopyEdit

sudo apt install ros-foxy-behaviortree-cpp-v3

2. Creating a Basic Behavior Tree in ROS2

First, create a simple **BT XML file** that defines a **decision-making hierarchy**.

Step 1: Writing a Behavior Tree XML File

xml

CopyEdit

```
<root main_tree_to_execute="MainTree">
```

```xml
<BehaviorTree ID="MainTree">

  <Sequence>

    <Condition ID="ObjectDetected"/>

    <Action ID="StopRobot"/>

    <Action ID="TurnLeft"/>

    <Action ID="MoveForward"/>

  </Sequence>

</BehaviorTree>

</root>
```

Step 2: Implementing ROS2 Nodes for Behavior Actions

Now, create C++ **action nodes** to implement the behaviors.

Condition Node (Check Object Detection)

cpp

CopyEdit

```cpp
class ObjectDetected : public BT::ConditionNode {

public:
```

```cpp
  ObjectDetected(const std::string& name) :
ConditionNode(name) {}

    BT::NodeStatus tick() override {

      bool detected = checkSensorData();  // Custom function

      return detected ? BT::NodeStatus::SUCCESS :
BT::NodeStatus::FAILURE;

    }

};
```

Action Node (Stop Robot)

cpp

CopyEdit

```cpp
class StopRobot : public BT::SyncActionNode {

public:

  StopRobot(const std::string& name) :
SyncActionNode(name, {}) {}

    BT::NodeStatus tick() override {

      stopMovement();  // Function to stop the robot
```

```cpp
    return BT::NodeStatus::SUCCESS;

  }

};
```

Action Node (Move Forward)

cpp

CopyEdit

```cpp
class MoveForward : public BT::SyncActionNode {
public:

  MoveForward(const std::string& name) :
SyncActionNode(name, {}) {}

  BT::NodeStatus tick() override {

    moveRobotForward();    // Function to command
movement

    return BT::NodeStatus::SUCCESS;

  }

};
```

Step 3: Running the Behavior Tree in ROS2

Compile and run the behavior tree in ROS2.

bash

CopyEdit

colcon build --packages-select my_behavior_tree

source install/setup.bash

ros2 run my_behavior_tree bt_runner

Developing a Robot That Detects and Reacts to Objects

Now, let's implement **a hands-on project** where the robot:

✅ **Detects an object** using LiDAR or a camera.

✅ **Stops movement when an object is detected**.

✅ **Turns left to avoid the obstacle**.

✅ **Continues navigating once the path is clear**.

1. Setting Up the Environment

Launching the Robot in Gazebo

bash

CopyEdit

```
ros2 launch turtlebot3_gazebo turtlebot3_world.launch.py
```

Starting the LiDAR Sensor Node

bash

CopyEdit

```
ros2 launch turtlebot3_bringup turtlebot3_lidar.launch.py
```

2. Implementing Object Detection in Python

Step 1: Subscribe to LiDAR Data

python

CopyEdit

```python
import rclpy

from rclpy.node import Node

from sensor_msgs.msg import LaserScan

from geometry_msgs.msg import Twist


class ObstacleAvoidance(Node):
```

```python
def __init__(self):

    super().__init__("obstacle_avoidance")

    self.publisher = self.create_publisher(Twist, "/cmd_vel", 10)

    self.subscription = self.create_subscription(LaserScan, "/scan", self.lidar_callback, 10)


def lidar_callback(self, msg):

    min_distance = min(msg.ranges)

    twist = Twist()


    if min_distance < 0.5:  # Object detected

        self.get_logger().info("Obstacle detected! Stopping.")

        twist.linear.x = 0.0

        twist.angular.z = 0.5  # Turn left

    else:

        twist.linear.x = 0.2  # Move forward
```

```python
        self.publisher.publish(twist)


rclpy.init()

node = ObstacleAvoidance()

rclpy.spin(node)
```

Chapter 7: Computer Vision and AI in Robotics

Imagine a world where robots can **see, interpret, and understand** their surroundings just like humans. Whether it's a self-driving car detecting pedestrians, a warehouse robot sorting packages, or a surgical robot identifying precise points for operation, **computer vision** is at the core of modern robotics.

For a robot to interact with the world, it must go beyond simple motion and navigation. It needs to **perceive, analyze, and respond** to visual information in real-time. **Computer vision**, powered by **Artificial Intelligence (AI)** and **Deep Learning**, enables robots to:

✅ **Recognize and track objects** in their environment.

✅ **Understand their surroundings** through depth perception and 3D mapping.

✅ **Make intelligent decisions** based on visual data.

✓ **Manipulate objects** by detecting shapes, sizes, and positions.

In this chapter, we will explore:

- **How robots see and process visual data.**

- **Techniques for object recognition, tracking, and environment awareness.**

- **Hands-on implementation of an object-picking robot using OpenCV and AI.**

- **Deep learning applications for advanced vision tasks.**

By the end of this chapter, you will have a solid understanding of **how to integrate computer vision into robotic systems** using **ROS2, OpenCV, and deep learning models**.

How Robots See and Process Visual Data

1. The Science Behind Robot Vision

At its core, **robot vision** is about capturing images and extracting meaningful information. Unlike human eyes, which process visual data intuitively, robots must rely on **cameras, sensors, and AI algorithms** to interpret their environment.

Key Components of Robot Vision:

Component	Function
Camera Sensors	Capture images or video (RGB, Depth, Infrared)
Image Processing	Enhances and filters raw image data
Feature Extraction	Identifies key patterns, edges, or objects
AI & Machine Learning	Recognizes and classifies objects using trained models
Robot Control System	Acts based on the visual information received

2. Types of Cameras Used in Robotics

Camera Type	Description	Use Cases
RGB Cameras	Standard color cameras that capture visible light.	Object recognition, navigation, and general vision tasks.
Depth Cameras	Use infrared or structured light to measure depth.	Obstacle avoidance, 3D mapping, and object grasping.
Stereo Cameras	Mimic human binocular vision to perceive depth.	SLAM (Simultaneous Localization and Mapping), 3D perception.
Thermal Cameras	Capture heat signatures instead of visible light.	Night vision, fire detection, security applications.
LiDAR Sensors	Use laser pulses to measure distances	Autonomous vehicles, drones, and

	and generate 3D maps.	environmental mapping.

Each type of camera plays a crucial role depending on the robotic application.

Object Recognition, Tracking, and Environment Awareness

1. Object Recognition in Robotics

Object recognition allows robots to identify specific objects in their environment using computer vision and AI models. This is essential for tasks such as:

✅ **Sorting objects in factories** (e.g., picking red apples from a conveyor belt).

✅ **Self-driving cars detecting traffic signs and pedestrians.**

✅ **Security robots identifying faces or unauthorized objects.**

Step 1: Implementing Object Recognition in ROS2 Using OpenCV

Install OpenCV if you haven't already:

bash

CopyEdit

pip install opencv-python

Create a ROS2 node for real-time object recognition using OpenCV:

python

CopyEdit

```python
import cv2

import rclpy

from rclpy.node import Node

from sensor_msgs.msg import Image

from cv_bridge import CvBridge


class ObjectRecognitionNode(Node):
    def __init__(self):
        super().__init__("object_recognition")
```

```python
        self.bridge = CvBridge()

        self.subscription    =    self.create_subscription(Image,
"/camera/image_raw", self.image_callback, 10)


    def image_callback(self, msg):

        frame = self.bridge.imgmsg_to_cv2(msg, "bgr8")

        gray = cv2.cvtColor(frame, cv2.COLOR_BGR2GRAY)

        objects = self.detect_objects(gray)

        for (x, y, w, h) in objects:

            cv2.rectangle(frame, (x, y), (x+w, y+h), (0, 255, 0), 2)


        cv2.imshow("Object Recognition", frame)

        cv2.waitKey(1)


    def detect_objects(self, frame):

        classifier = cv2.CascadeClassifier(cv2.data.haarcascades
+ "haarcascade_frontalface_default.xml")
```

```
return                    classifier.detectMultiScale(frame,
scaleFactor=1.1, minNeighbors=5)
```

```
rclpy.init()

node = ObjectRecognitionNode()

rclpy.spin(node)
```

This script **detects objects** (e.g., faces) in real-time using OpenCV in a ROS2 environment.

2. Object Tracking in Robotics

Object tracking is essential when robots need to follow or interact with moving objects. This is crucial for:

✅ **Autonomous drones tracking people or vehicles.**

✅ **Warehouse robots following inventory items.**

✅ **Surveillance robots monitoring moving objects.**

Implementing Object Tracking in ROS2

We can use **OpenCV's tracking API** to track objects dynamically.

```python
CopyEdit
import cv2
import rclpy
from rclpy.node import Node
from sensor_msgs.msg import Image
from cv_bridge import CvBridge


class ObjectTrackingNode(Node):
    def __init__(self):
        super().__init__("object_tracking")
        self.bridge = CvBridge()
        self.subscription = self.create_subscription(Image, "/camera/image_raw", self.image_callback, 10)
        self.tracker = cv2.TrackerKCF_create()
        self.initBB = None  # Bounding box
```

```python
def image_callback(self, msg):

    frame = self.bridge.imgmsg_to_cv2(msg, "bgr8")


    if self.initBB is not None:

        success, box = self.tracker.update(frame)
        if success:

            (x, y, w, h) = [int(v) for v in box]

            cv2.rectangle(frame, (x, y), (x+w, y+h), (0, 255, 0), 2)


    cv2.imshow("Object Tracking", frame)

    cv2.waitKey(1)


rclpy.init()

node = ObjectTrackingNode()

rclpy.spin(node)
```

Building an Object-Picking Robot with OpenCV and AI

1. How Object Picking Works

To enable a robot to **pick and place objects**, we must:

1. **Detect the object** using OpenCV.

2. **Determine the object's position** using depth sensors.

3. **Control a robotic arm** to pick the object.

Step 1: Detecting and Locating the Object

python

CopyEdit

```
object_cascade = cv2.CascadeClassifier('object_cascade.xml')

gray = cv2.cvtColor(frame, cv2.COLOR_BGR2GRAY)

objects = object_cascade.detectMultiScale(gray, 1.3, 5)


for (x, y, w, h) in objects:

    cv2.rectangle(frame, (x, y), (x + w, y + h), (0, 255, 0), 2)

    object_center = (x + w//2, y + h//2)
```

Step 2: Moving the Robot Arm to Pick the Object

python

CopyEdit

```python
from moveit_commander import RobotCommander, MoveGroupCommander

robot = RobotCommander()

group = MoveGroupCommander("arm")

group.set_pose_target(object_pose)

group.go(wait=True)
```

This enables a **robotic arm to pick objects** accurately based on **computer vision**.

Deep Learning Applications for Advanced Vision Tasks

Deep learning significantly enhances computer vision tasks like:

✅ **Face and gesture recognition**.

✅ **Scene segmentation and 3D reconstruction**.

✅ **Autonomous object classification and grasping**.

Using YOLO for Object Detection in ROS2

python

CopyEdit

```
import torch

model = torch.hub.load('ultralytics/yolov5', 'yolov5s')

results = model(frame)

results.show()
```

This allows robots to **detect multiple objects** with high accuracy.

Chapter 8: Robot Manipulation and Dexterous Control

Robotic manipulation is one of the **most complex yet essential** capabilities in robotics. The ability to **grasp, pick, move, and interact** with objects enables robots to perform **manufacturing, logistics, medical, and even space exploration tasks**. From robotic arms on assembly lines to robotic-assisted surgeries, **dexterous control** is crucial in real world robotic applications.

In this chapter, we will explore:

✅ **How robotic arms function and achieve precision control.**

✅ **Programming robotic manipulation using ROS2 and MoveIt!.**

✅ **Grasping, picking, and placing objects with AI-assisted control.**

✓ **Hands-on project: Developing a functional robotic arm using ROS2**.

By the end of this chapter, you will have a **deep understanding of robot arm kinematics, path planning, and real-world robotic manipulation techniques**.

Understanding Robotic Arms and Precision Control

1. Anatomy of a Robotic Arm

Robotic arms consist of multiple **joints and links**, allowing them to move **in precise and coordinated ways**. Key components include:

Component	Function
Base	Fixed or rotating foundation of the robotic arm.
Joints	Rotational or prismatic (linear) movement points.
Links	Connect joints to form the structure of the arm.
End Effector	The tool at the arm's end (gripper, suction cup, welding torch).
Actuators	Motors responsible for movement and force application.
Sensors	Provide feedback on position, force, and surroundings.

2. Forward and Inverse Kinematics

Kinematics is the study of how a robotic arm moves.

- **Forward Kinematics (FK)**: Given joint angles, calculates the **end effector's position**.

- **Inverse Kinematics (IK)**: Given a desired **end effector position**, determines the necessary **joint angles**.

Example: Using **MoveIt!** in ROS2 to solve inverse kinematics.

python

CopyEdit

```
from moveit_commander import RobotCommander, MoveGroupCommander


robot = RobotCommander()

group = MoveGroupCommander("manipulator")


# Define target position

target_pose = group.get_current_pose()

target_pose.pose.position.x = 0.4
```

target_pose.pose.position.y = 0.2

target_pose.pose.position.z = 0.5

group.set_pose_target(target_pose)

group.go(wait=True)

3. Degrees of Freedom (DoF) in Robotic Arms

The **number of independent movements** a robotic arm can perform is known as its **Degrees of Freedom (DoF)**.

Arm Type	DoF	Examples
2-DoF Arm	2	Simple robotic grippers
4-DoF Arm	4	Basic pick-and-place robots
6-DoF Arm	6	Industrial and surgical robots
7-DoF Arm	7	Highly dexterous robotic manipulators (e.g., human-like arms)

Higher **DoF allows for greater flexibility and dexterity**, enabling robots to perform **complex, human-like movements**.

Programming Robotic Manipulation with ROS2 and MoveIt!

1. Introduction to MoveIt! for Motion Planning

MoveIt! is **ROS2's primary tool** for robotic arm control, providing:

✓ **Motion planning** (finding paths without collisions).

✓ **Inverse kinematics** (determining joint angles for target positions).

✓ **Obstacle avoidance**.

✓ **Grasping and object manipulation**.

2. Setting Up MoveIt! in ROS2

Installing MoveIt!

bash

CopyEdit

```
sudo apt install ros-foxy-moveit
```

Launching MoveIt!

bash

CopyEdit

```
ros2 launch moveit2 move_group.launch.py
```

3. Controlling a Robot Arm with MoveIt! in ROS2

Step 1: Move the End Effector to a Target Position

python

CopyEdit

```
group.set_named_target("home")

group.go(wait=True)
```

Step 2: Plan a Path to a New Position

python

CopyEdit

```
target_pose.pose.position.x = 0.5

target_pose.pose.position.y = 0.0

target_pose.pose.position.z = 0.3

group.set_pose_target(target_pose)

plan = group.plan()

group.execute(plan, wait=True)
```

Step 3: Avoid Obstacles During Motion Planning

python

CopyEdit

from moveit_commander import PlanningSceneInterface

scene = PlanningSceneInterface()

scene.add_box("obstacle", size=(0.1, 0.1, 0.1), pose=[0.4, 0, 0.5])

Now the robot will **automatically re-route** to avoid the obstacle while reaching its goal.

Grasping, Picking, and Placing Objects with AI-Assisted Control

1. Object Grasping Using Depth Perception

For robots to **pick and place objects**, they must first:

1. **Detect the object's position using a camera or LiDAR.**

2. **Calculate the best grasping angle and approach.**

3. **Control the robotic arm to pick the object.**

4. **Transport and place the object in a target location.**

Example: **Using OpenCV and AI for Object Detection in ROS2**

python

CopyEdit

```python
import cv2

import rclpy

from sensor_msgs.msg import Image

from cv_bridge import CvBridge


class ObjectDetection(Node):
    def __init__(self):
        super().__init__("object_detection")
        self.bridge = CvBridge()
```

```python
        self.subscription    =    self.create_subscription(Image,
"/camera/image_raw", self.image_callback, 10)


    def image_callback(self, msg):

        frame = self.bridge.imgmsg_to_cv2(msg, "bgr8")

        gray = cv2.cvtColor(frame, cv2.COLOR_BGR2GRAY)

        objects                                               =
cv2.CascadeClassifier('object_cascade.xml').detectMultiScale
(gray, 1.1, 4)


        for (x, y, w, h) in objects:

            cv2.rectangle(frame, (x, y), (x + w, y + h), (0, 255, 0),
2)


        cv2.imshow("Object Detection", frame)

        cv2.waitKey(1)


rclpy.init()
```

```
node = ObjectDetection()

rclpy.spin(node)
```

2. AI-Assisted Grasping with Deep Learning

Neural networks allow robots to **identify optimal grasp points** for objects.

✅ **YOLO-based object detection** for **real-time grasping.**

✅ **Reinforcement learning** to improve **robotic dexterity.**

Example: **Using YOLO for AI-Assisted Object Recognition**

python

CopyEdit

```
import torch

model = torch.hub.load('ultralytics/yolov5', 'yolov5s')

results = model(frame)

results.show()
```

Hands-on Project: Developing a Functional Robotic Arm

Project Overview

Goal: **Build a ROS2-powered robotic arm that can pick up objects, move them, and place them in a designated location.**

Step 1: Setting Up the Robot Arm in MoveIt!

bash

CopyEdit

```
ros2 launch moveit2 move_group.launch.py
```

Step 2: Programming Pick-and-Place Actions

python

CopyEdit

```
from moveit_commander import RobotCommander, MoveGroupCommander


robot = RobotCommander()
```

```python
group = MoveGroupCommander("arm")

# Pick Position
pick_pose = group.get_current_pose()
pick_pose.pose.position.x = 0.2
pick_pose.pose.position.y = -0.1
pick_pose.pose.position.z = 0.3

group.set_pose_target(pick_pose)
group.go(wait=True)

# Grasp the object
gripper_group = MoveGroupCommander("gripper")
gripper_group.set_named_target("closed")
gripper_group.go(wait=True)

# Move to place position
```

```python
place_pose = pick_pose

place_pose.pose.position.y += 0.3

group.set_pose_target(place_pose)

group.go(wait=True)


# Release the object

gripper_group.set_named_target("open")

gripper_group.go(wait=True)
```

Chapter 9: Human-Robot Interaction and Speech Recognition

Imagine a world where robots seamlessly assist humans—whether by responding to voice commands, recognizing facial expressions, or even understanding social cues. From AI-powered home assistants to robotic caregivers, **Human-Robot Interaction (HRI)** is transforming the way machines integrate into daily life.

HRI is a multidisciplinary field combining **robotics, artificial intelligence, psychology, and human-computer interaction** to create systems that interact **naturally and intuitively** with people. The ability of robots to understand **speech, gestures, and emotions** is crucial for their adoption in environments like homes, hospitals, and workplaces.

What We Will Cover in This Chapter

- The **principles of natural and intuitive human-robot interaction** (HRI).

- How to **build robots that understand speech and gestures** using AI and ROS2.

- The **role of social and assistive robotics** in healthcare and beyond.

By the end of this chapter, you will understand **how to design, develop, and implement human-friendly robots** that respond intelligently to verbal and non-verbal cues.

Principles of Natural and Intuitive Human-Robot Interaction

1. Understanding Human-Robot Interaction (HRI)

Human-Robot Interaction (HRI) focuses on creating **intuitive, seamless, and meaningful** interactions between humans and robots.

Type of Interaction	Description	Examples
Verbal Communication	Robots understand and respond to spoken language.	Voice assistants, call center AI, robot tutors.
Non-Verbal Communication	Robots interpret gestures, facial expressions, and body language.	Gesture-controlled drones, facial recognition security.
Tactile Interaction	Robots respond to touch or haptic feedback.	Robotic prosthetics, robotic pets.

Emotional Intelligence	AI-driven robots detect and respond to human emotions.	Social companion robots, therapy robots.

A well-designed HRI system should:

✅ **Be intuitive and easy to use** (minimal learning curve).

✅ **Adapt to different users** (children, elderly, disabled individuals).

✅ **Offer real-time feedback** (acknowledge user actions).

✅ **Be culturally and socially aware** (avoid misinterpretations).

2. Challenges in Human-Robot Interaction

Despite advancements, HRI faces several **technical and ethical** challenges:

Challenge	Explanation

Speech Recognition Accuracy	Accents, background noise, and ambiguous phrases can confuse AI.
Gesture Recognition Limitations	Variability in human gestures makes it hard to define precise movements.
Emotional Misinterpretation	AI struggles with subtle emotional cues.
Privacy and Ethics	Robots collecting personal data raise security concerns.
Trust and Acceptance	Some users may feel uneasy interacting with robots.

To tackle these challenges, **AI-driven adaptive learning** and **better sensor fusion** techniques are being integrated into modern robots.

Building Robots That Understand Speech and Gestures

1. Speech Recognition in Robotics

Speech recognition allows robots to **understand and execute voice commands**. Modern systems use **Natural Language Processing (NLP) and Deep Learning** to improve accuracy.

Popular Speech Recognition Libraries:

- **Google Speech API** – Cloud-based, highly accurate.

- **CMU Sphinx** – Open-source, works offline.

- **DeepSpeech by Mozilla** – Deep learning-powered speech recognition.

Installing Speech Recognition in ROS2

To enable speech processing, install **SpeechRecognition** and **PyAudio**:

bash

CopyEdit

pip install SpeechRecognition pyaudio

Step 1: Implementing Basic Speech Recognition in ROS2

python

CopyEdit

```python
import rclpy
import speech_recognition as sr
from rclpy.node import Node

class SpeechRecognitionNode(Node):
    def __init__(self):
        super().__init__("speech_recognition")
        self.recognizer = sr.Recognizer()
        self.microphone = sr.Microphone()
        self.timer = self.create_timer(5.0, self.recognize_speech)

    def recognize_speech(self):
        with self.microphone as source:
            self.get_logger().info("Listening for a command...")
            audio = self.recognizer.listen(source)
```

```
try:

    command = self.recognizer.recognize_google(audio)

    self.get_logger().info(f"Recognized          Command:
{command}")

    except sr.UnknownValueError:

    self.get_logger().info("Could not understand speech")

    except sr.RequestError:

    self.get_logger().info("Speech    recognition    service
unavailable")


rclpy.init()

node = SpeechRecognitionNode()

rclpy.spin(node)
```

This script:

✅ **Listens for speech.**

✅ **Processes the audio input.**

✅ **Recognizes commands using Google Speech API.**

2. Gesture Recognition in Robotics

Gesture recognition allows robots to interpret **hand signals and body movements**, making interactions **more natural**.

Popular Gesture Recognition Technologies

- **OpenPose** – AI-powered human motion tracking.

- **MediaPipe** – Google's gesture detection framework.

- **Leap Motion** – Tracks hand and finger movements.

Step 2: Implementing Hand Gesture Recognition with OpenCV

python

CopyEdit

```
import cv2
import mediapipe as mp


mp_hands = mp.solutions.hands
hands = mp_hands.Hands()
mp_drawing = mp.solutions.drawing_utils
```

```python
cap = cv2.VideoCapture(0)

while cap.isOpened():

    success, frame = cap.read()

    if not success:

        break


    rgb_frame                =                cv2.cvtColor(frame,
cv2.COLOR_BGR2RGB)

    result = hands.process(rgb_frame)


    if result.multi_hand_landmarks:

        for hand_landmarks in result.multi_hand_landmarks:

            mp_drawing.draw_landmarks(frame,
hand_landmarks, mp_hands.HAND_CONNECTIONS)


    cv2.imshow("Hand Gesture Recognition", frame)
```

```
if cv2.waitKey(1) & 0xFF == ord("q"):

    break
```

```
cap.release()
```

```
cv2.destroyAllWindows()
```

This   script:

✓   Uses   **MediaPipe**   to   detect   hands.

✓ Tracks **hand landmarks** for gesture recognition.

3. Combining Speech and Gesture Control in ROS2

We can integrate **speech and gesture commands** to make robots more interactive.

Example: Controlling a Robot with Both Speech and Gestures

python

CopyEdit

```
if command == "move forward":
```

```
send_robot_command("forward")

elif gesture == "thumbs up":

    send_robot_command("start")
```

By combining **AI-powered speech and vision**, robots can interact with humans in **more natural ways**.

The Role of Social and Assistive Robotics in Healthcare and Beyond

Social and assistive robotics are revolutionizing **healthcare, education, and companionship**.

1. Healthcare Robotics

✓ **Elderly Assistance** – Robots like **Paro the Seal** provide emotional   support.

✓ **Surgical Robots** – **da Vinci** robot enhances precision in surgeries.

✓ **Physical Therapy Robots** – Help patients recover through guided exercises.

Example: AI-Assisted Patient Monitoring

python

CopyEdit

```
if detected_face == "elderly_person" and mood ==
"distressed":
    alert_caregiver()
```

2. Educational and Companion Robots

✅ **AI tutors** – Pepper robot helps children learn languages.

✅ **Autism therapy robots** – NAO robot helps children with autism communicate.

Example: Robot Tutor with Speech Interaction

python

CopyEdit

```
if user_says("what is 2+2"):
    robot_reply("The answer is 4.")
```

3. Ethical Considerations in Social Robotics

Concern	Solution
Privacy Risks	Ensure encrypted data storage and anonymization.
AI Bias in Interaction	Train models on diverse datasets.
Human Dependence	Encourage hybrid human-AI collaboration.

As robots become **more human-like**, it is essential to design them **ethically and responsibly**.

Chapter 10: Building a Fully Functional Autonomous Robot

Building a fully functional **autonomous robot** is one of the most exciting and challenging tasks in robotics. It requires integrating **hardware, sensors, AI, and motion control** to create a system capable of making **intelligent decisions in real-world environments**.

In this chapter, we will explore:

✅ **Choosing the right hardware for your DIY robot project.**

✅ **Assembling and testing an intelligent robot system.**

✅ **Combining AI, sensors, and motion control for real-world automation.**

By the end of this chapter, you will have the **knowledge and hands-on experience** needed to build an autonomous robot capable of navigating, sensing, and performing intelligent tasks.

Choosing the Right Hardware for Your DIY Robot Project

1. Selecting the Robot's Core Components

An autonomous robot consists of several key components:

Component	Function	Examples
Microcontroller/Processor	The brain of the robot, processes data and controls actions	Raspberry Pi, NVIDIA Jetson Nano, Arduino
Sensors	Provide environmental awareness	LiDAR, Cameras, IMU, Ultrasonic sensors
Motors & Actuators	Enable movement and interaction	DC motors, Servo motors,

		Stepper motors
Power System	Provides energy to the robot	LiPo Battery, Rechargeabl e NiMH, Power banks
Communication Modules	Allows wireless control and data transmission	Wi-Fi, Bluetooth, LoRa, Zigbee

2. Choosing a Microcontroller or Single-Board Computer (SBC)

Microcontrollers vs. Single-Board Computers

Feature	Microcontroller (e.g., Arduino)	Single-Board Computer (e.g., Raspberry Pi, Jetson Nano)

Processing Power	Low	High
Operating System	None (Runs simple code)	Linux-based (Can run ROS2, AI models)
Connectivity	Limited (Serial, I2C, SPI)	Wi-Fi, Bluetooth, Ethernet
Use Case	Simple robotic projects (line-following robot)	AI-powered robots (autonomous navigation, deep learning)

For an **AI-powered autonomous robot, Raspberry Pi 4** or **NVIDIA Jetson Nano** is recommended because they support **ROS2, computer vision, and AI processing**.

Example: Installing ROS2 on Raspberry Pi

bash

CopyEdit

sudo apt update

sudo apt install ros-foxy-desktop

3. Selecting the Right Sensors

For autonomy, the robot must perceive its surroundings accurately using **multiple sensors**:

Sensor Type	Function	Use Cases
LiDAR (Light Detection and Ranging)	Measures distance using laser beams	SLAM, Obstacle detection
Camera (RGB, Depth, IR)	Captures visual data for processing	Object recognition, Navigation
IMU (Inertial Measurement Unit)	Detects orientation, acceleration	Self-balancing robots, Drones
Ultrasonic Sensors	Uses sound waves to detect objects	Short-range obstacle detection

GPS (Global Positioning System)	Provides location data	Outdoor navigation

Example: Integrating LiDAR with ROS2

bash

CopyEdit

```
ros2 launch rplidar_ros rplidar.launch.py
```

4. Choosing the Right Motors and Actuators

The robot's movement depends on **motor selection**:

Motor Type	Function	Example Applications
DC Motors	Continuous rotation, speed control	Wheeled robots, mobile bases
Servo Motors	Precise angular movement	Robot arms, pan-tilt camera

Stepper Motors	Precise step-based rotation	3D printers, CNC machines

Motor Control Using ROS2:

python

CopyEdit

```
import rclpy

from geometry_msgs.msg import Twist


node = rclpy.create_node("motor_control")
pub = node.create_publisher(Twist, "/cmd_vel", 10)


twist = Twist()
twist.linear.x = 0.5  # Move forward
twist.angular.z = 0.2  # Turn slightly
pub.publish(twist)
```

Assembling and Testing an Intelligent Robot System

1. Building the Robot's Physical Structure

Steps for Assembly:

✅ **Design the robot chassis** (using 3D printing or aluminum frame).

✅ **Attach the motors and wheels** (ensure proper motor alignment).

✅ **Mount the sensors** (LiDAR, cameras, IMU).

✅ **Secure the power supply** (battery pack with voltage regulator).

✅ **Install the microcontroller/SBC** (connect all components to it).

Example: Wiring an Arduino-Based Robot

1. **Connect DC motors to an H-Bridge motor driver**.
2. **Attach sensors to appropriate GPIO pins**.

3. **Power the system with a LiPo battery and voltage regulator**.

2. Setting Up the Robot's Software Framework

For intelligent behavior, the robot's **software stack** should include:

☑ **ROS2 for communication and sensor fusion.**

☑ **SLAM (Simultaneous Localization and Mapping) for navigation.**

☑ **AI models for object detection and decision-making.**

Installing ROS2 Navigation Stack

bash

CopyEdit

```
sudo apt install ros-foxy-navigation2

ros2 launch nav2_bringup navigation_launch.py
```

3. Testing and Debugging the Robot

Before deploying the robot, **test all components individually**:

Component	Test Procedure
Motors	Send commands and check movement.
Sensors	Verify data streaming (e.g., LiDAR visualization in RViz).
Camera	Capture and display frames using OpenCV.
Power System	Ensure stable voltage levels.

Example: Testing LiDAR Data in RViz

bash

CopyEdit

ros2 launch rplidar_ros rplidar.launch.py

ros2 run rviz2 rviz2

Combining AI, Sensors, and Motion for Real-World Automation

1. Implementing SLAM for Navigation

SLAM (Simultaneous Localization and Mapping) allows robots to:

☑ **Create a map of their environment**.

☑ **Localize themselves in real-time**.

☑ **Navigate autonomously without GPS**.

Running SLAM in ROS2

bash

CopyEdit

```
ros2 launch slam_toolbox online_async_launch.py
```

2. AI-Powered Object Detection for Smart Navigation

For AI-driven automation, robots must recognize and **react to objects dynamically**.

Example: Using YOLO for Object Detection

python

CopyEdit

import torch

model = torch.hub.load('ultralytics/yolov5', 'yolov5s')

results = model('test_image.jpg')

results.show()

3. Implementing Autonomous Path Planning

Once a robot **understands its surroundings**, it must navigate efficiently using **path planning algorithms**.

Algorithm	Use Case
A*	Finds shortest path in structured environments
Dijkstra's Algorithm	Guarantees shortest path in all cases
RRT (Rapidly Exploring Random Trees)	Used for complex obstacle avoidance

Running Path Planning in ROS2

bash

CopyEdit

```
ros2 action send_goal /navigate_to_pose nav2_msgs/action/NavigateToPose "{pose: {position: {x: 1.0, y: 2.0}}}"
```

Hands-On Project: Building a Fully Autonomous Robot

Step 1: Setting Up the Robot in Gazebo

bash

CopyEdit

```bash
ros2 launch gazebo_ros empty_world.launch.py
```

Step 2: Integrating SLAM and Navigation

bash

CopyEdit

```bash
ros2 launch slam_toolbox online_async_launch.py

ros2 launch nav2_bringup navigation_launch.py
```

Step 3: Adding AI Object Detection

python

CopyEdit

```python
if detected_object == "person":

    stop_robot()

elif detected_object == "door":
```

navigate_through_door()

Step 4: Testing the Robot in a Real Environment

✅ **Check sensor accuracy.**

✅ **Validate AI-based decision-making.**

✅ **Ensure smooth obstacle avoidance.**

Chapter 11: Debugging and Troubleshooting Robotics Systems

Developing an autonomous robot is a challenging but rewarding process. However, even the most well-designed robotic systems can encounter **unexpected failures, communication breakdowns, sensor malfunctions, or software crashes**. Debugging these issues effectively is a crucial skill for any roboticist.

Debugging in robotics is more complex than traditional software debugging because it involves **hardware, sensors, networking, real-time processing, and AI integration**. A single issue might stem from **mechanical faults, electrical wiring problems, software bugs, or environmental factors**.

In this chapter, we will explore:

- **Common challenges in robot development and deployment**.

- **Effective debugging techniques for ROS2 and Python-based robotic systems**.

- **Remote debugging and performance optimization strategies** to ensure stable robot operation.

By the end of this chapter, you will have a **systematic approach to identifying, diagnosing, and resolving problems in autonomous robotic systems**.

Common Challenges in Robot Development and Deployment

Robotics is a **multidisciplinary field** combining **software, electronics, and mechanical systems**. Each component introduces its own set of challenges.

1. Hardware and Electrical Issues

Problem	Possible Causes	Solution
Motors not moving	Loose wiring, incorrect voltage, or faulty motor drivers	Check power connections, use a multimeter to measure voltage
Sensor data fluctuating wildly	Electrical noise, poor sensor placement	Use shielded cables, add signal filtering, reposition sensors
Battery drains too fast	Incorrect power management	Optimize power consumption, use energy-efficient motors

Microcontroller overheating	Poor ventilation, excessive power draw	Improve heat dissipation, check voltage regulation

Example: Diagnosing Motor Control Issues in ROS2

python

CopyEdit

```python
import rclpy

from geometry_msgs.msg import Twist


def check_motor_connection():

    node = rclpy.create_node("motor_diagnostic")

    pub = node.create_publisher(Twist, "/cmd_vel", 10)


    test_signal = Twist()

    test_signal.linear.x = 0.5  # Move forward

    pub.publish(test_signal)

    node.get_logger().info("Sent test signal to motors")
```

rclpy.init()

check_motor_connection()

If the robot doesn't move, check motor driver connections and power supply.

2. Software and ROS2 Communication Issues

ROS2 relies on **nodes, topics, services, and actions** to manage robot communication. Common software issues include:

Issue	Cause	Solution
Nodes not launching	Incorrect package installation, missing dependencies	Run ros2 doctor to check system health
Topic data not being received	Publisher and subscriber misconfigured	Use ros2 topic list and ros2 topic echo to verify data flow
Service calls failing	Incorrect request format	Use ros2 service list and ros2

		service type to debug
Robot lagging or freezing	Inefficient processing, overloaded CPU	Profile CPU usage with htop and optimize code

Example: Checking ROS2 Topics

bash

CopyEdit

ros2 topic list

ros2 topic echo /sensor_data

If the expected data is not appearing, verify that the **publisher node is running correctly**.

3. Sensor and Perception Challenges

Robots rely on sensors like **LiDAR, cameras, IMUs, and ultrasonic sensors**. Issues often arise due to **calibration errors, sensor noise, or incorrect data interpretation**.

Problem	Cause	Solution

LiDAR missing obstacles	Incorrect sensor mounting	Adjust sensor angle, recalibrate LiDAR
Depth camera not detecting objects	Incorrect lighting, bad calibration	Reconfigure exposure settings, recalibrate using OpenCV
IMU drift over time	Sensor noise, incorrect filtering	Apply sensor fusion techniques like Kalman filters

Example: Checking LiDAR Data in ROS2

bash

CopyEdit

```
ros2 run rviz2 rviz2
```

If the LiDAR scan is incomplete, check for **sensor obstructions or loose connections**.

Effective Debugging Techniques for ROS2 and Python

Debugging in ROS2 involves **systematic testing, logging, and visualization tools**. Here's a structured approach to solving common problems.

1. Using ROS2 Logging for Debugging

ROS2 provides built-in logging to track errors and warnings.

Setting Log Levels

python

CopyEdit

```
node.get_logger().info("This is an informational message.")

node.get_logger().warn("This is a warning.")

node.get_logger().error("This is an error message!")
```

Viewing Logs in ROS2

bash

CopyEdit

```
ros2 log list
```

ros2 log info

This helps **identify crashes and runtime issues** in ROS2 nodes.

2. Debugging ROS2 Nodes and Topics

Step 1: Check if all nodes are running properly

bash

CopyEdit

```
ros2 node list

ros2 node info /my_robot_node
```

Step 2: Verify if the robot is publishing the right messages

bash

CopyEdit

```
ros2 topic list

ros2 topic echo /cmd_vel
```

Step 3: Test service calls

bash

CopyEdit

ros2 service list

ros2 service call /restart_robot std_srvs/srv/Empty

If these commands **return unexpected results**, investigate the node's **launch file, message types, or callback functions**.

3. Using Debugging Tools for Python in Robotics

Enabling Debug Mode in Python

python

CopyEdit

```
import pdb


def debug_function():
    x = 10
    pdb.set_trace()  # Debug breakpoint
    y = x + 5
    print(y)
```

debug_function()

Profiling Code Performance in ROS2

python

CopyEdit

import cProfile

def expensive_function():

   for i in range(1000000):

      pass

cProfile.run('expensive_function()')

This helps **identify bottlenecks** in Python scripts running inside ROS2 nodes.

Remote Debugging and Performance Optimization Strategies

1. Debugging a Robot Remotely Using SSH

If your robot is deployed in a remote environment, debugging via **SSH (Secure Shell)** is essential.

Connecting to the Robot

bash

CopyEdit

```
ssh user@robot_ip_address
```

Once connected, run ROS2 debugging tools remotely.

2. Monitoring CPU and Memory Usage on a Robot

Heavy processing tasks (e.g., AI models, SLAM) can cause **CPU overload**. Use htop to monitor performance.

Installing and Running htop

bash

CopyEdit

sudo apt install htop

htop

Look for **high CPU or RAM usage** and optimize accordingly.

3. Optimizing ROS2 Performance

Optimization	Description
Use Efficient Data Types	Avoid excessive message sizes (e.g., compress images before sending).
Reduce Unnecessary Computations	Minimize loops and redundant processing.
Adjust ROS2 QoS Settings	Improve message reliability using **best-effort** mode for non-critical data.
Use ROS2 Bags for Data Analysis	Record sensor data and analyze logs offline.

Example: Using ROS2 Bags for Debugging

bash

CopyEdit

```
ros2 bag record -a
```

Later, replay the recorded data:

bash

CopyEdit

```
ros2 bag play <bag_file>
```

Chapter 12: The Future of Robotics and AI Integration

The field of robotics is undergoing a **revolution** powered by **Artificial Intelligence (AI), machine learning (ML), cloud computing, and swarm intelligence**. Robots are evolving from **pre-programmed machines** to **adaptive, learning-based systems** that can perceive, reason, and interact **autonomously**.

As AI continues to advance, we are witnessing the emergence of **next-generation robots** that can:

✅ **Learn from experience** and adapt to new tasks.

✅ **Work together using swarm intelligence**.

✅ **Leverage cloud computing** for real-time processing and decision-making.

✅ **Interact ethically and safely with humans**.

In this chapter, we will explore:

- **How AI and machine learning will shape next-gen robots.**

- **Cloud robotics, swarm intelligence, and the future of robot collaboration.**

- **Ethical considerations and the role of safe AI in robotics.**

By the end of this chapter, you will have a **deep understanding of where robotics is headed** and how AI will continue to **shape the future of automation**.

How AI and Machine Learning Will Shape Next-Gen Robots

1. The Role of AI in Modern Robotics

Artificial Intelligence is transforming robotics by **enabling robots to perceive, analyze, and act intelligently**. Traditional robots followed **fixed rules** and were **limited to repetitive tasks**, but AI-powered robots can now:

◆ **Recognize objects and people** using deep learning.

◆ **Understand and process human speech** using NLP (Natural Language Processing).

◆ **Make autonomous decisions** based on real-time data.

◆ **Adapt to new environments** through reinforcement learning.

AI Capability	Application in Robotics
Computer Vision	Object detection, facial recognition, autonomous driving

Natural Language Processing (NLP)	Human-robot interaction, speech assistants
Reinforcement Learning	Adaptive motion control, robot decision-making
Generative AI	Simulating environments, creating new robot behaviors

2. Machine Learning Techniques Used in Robotics

AI-powered robots use different **machine learning techniques** to improve performance.

ML Technique	How It Works	Example Use Cases
Supervised Learning	The robot learns from labeled data	Identifying defective products in manufacturing
Unsupervised Learning	The robot finds patterns in unlabeled data	Grouping similar objects in warehouse sorting

Reinforcement Learning (RL)	The robot learns through trial and error	Teaching a robot dog to walk on rough terrain
Deep Learning (Neural Networks)	AI mimics the human brain to recognize patterns	Self-driving cars detecting pedestrians

Example: Training a Robot to Recognize Objects Using Deep Learning

python

CopyEdit

import torch

from torchvision import models, transforms

from PIL import Image

model = models.resnet50(pretrained=True)

model.eval()

```python
image = Image.open("object.jpg")

transform = transforms.Compose([

    transforms.Resize((224, 224)),

    transforms.ToTensor()

])


img_tensor = transform(image).unsqueeze(0)

output = model(img_tensor)

predicted_class = torch.argmax(output).item()


print(f"Predicted Object: {predicted_class}")
```

3. AI-Powered Autonomous Robots

The next generation of robots will be **fully autonomous,** capable of making decisions **without human intervention**.

Real-World Examples of AI-Powered Autonomous Robots

☐ **Tesla's Optimus** – A humanoid robot designed for industrial automation.

🚗 **Waymo's Self-Driving Cars** – AI-powered autonomous vehicles using reinforcement learning.

⊕ **Da Vinci Surgical Robot** – AI-assisted surgery with extreme precision.

📦 **Amazon Robotics** – Warehouse robots using AI for logistics and inventory management.

With AI, robots can **move beyond static automation and enter dynamic, unpredictable environments** like hospitals, disaster zones, and smart cities.

Cloud Robotics, Swarm Intelligence, and the Future of Collaboration

1. Cloud Robotics: The Power of Internet-Connected Robots

Cloud robotics is an **emerging field** where robots **offload processing tasks to the cloud** instead of relying solely on onboard hardware.

Benefits of Cloud Robotics:

✅ **Computational Efficiency** – Offload heavy AI tasks to cloud servers.

✅ **Real-Time Data Sharing** – Robots can share experiences and improve collaboratively.

✅ **Scalability** – Robots can be updated with new skills remotely.

Example: Connecting a Robot to the Cloud Using ROS2

python

CopyEdit

import requests

```
cloud_url = "https://cloud-robot-server.com/api"

data = {"robot_status": "active"}


response = requests.post(cloud_url, json=data)

print(f"Cloud Response: {response.json()}")
```

Cloud-based AI enables robots to **process complex data instantly**, making them more adaptable in real-world environments.

2. Swarm Intelligence: How Robots Work Together

Swarm robotics is inspired by **nature**—just as **ants, bees, and birds coordinate movements**, robots can work together **without centralized control**.

Applications of Swarm Robotics:

✅ **Disaster Response** – Drones mapping disaster sites in real-time.

✅ **Agriculture** – Swarm robots monitoring crop health.

✅ **Warehouse Automation** – Hundreds of robots sorting and delivering packages.

Example: Simulating a Swarm of Robots in ROS2

python

CopyEdit

```
from swarm_robotics import Swarm

swarm = Swarm(num_robots=10)

swarm.simulate()
```

3. The Future of Human-Robot Collaboration

In the future, humans and robots will **work side by side**, improving productivity and safety.

Industry	Future Robot Applications
Healthcare	AI-powered surgical assistants, robotic caregivers
Manufacturing	Smart factory robots collaborating with humans

Retail	AI checkout robots, automated inventory tracking
Education	AI tutors and learning assistants

Collaborative robots (**cobots**) will help industries become more **efficient and adaptable**, reducing human labor in dangerous tasks.

Ethical Considerations and the Role of Safe AI in Robotics

As AI and robotics become more advanced, ethical concerns arise. How do we ensure that robots **benefit humanity while minimizing risks**?

1. The Ethical Dilemmas of AI in Robotics

Ethical Issue	Challenge	Possible Solutions
Job Displacement	AI replacing human jobs	Focus on human-AI collaboration

Bias in AI	AI can inherit biases from training data	Use diverse, unbiased datasets
Privacy Concerns	Robots collecting sensitive data	Implement strict data security laws
Robot Autonomy & Control	Preventing harmful robot decisions	Human oversight & regulation

One of the most debated topics is **AI in military robotics**—should we allow robots to make **life-or-death decisions**?

2. Ensuring Safe AI in Robotics

To develop safe and ethical AI-powered robots, we need:

◆ **Explainable AI (XAI)** – Making AI decisions transparent.

◆ **Regulatory Policies** – Governments must create **AI safety laws**.

◆ **Human-in-the-Loop Systems** – Ensure human oversight in high-risk applications.

- ♦ **Fail-Safe Mechanisms** – Implement emergency stop functions in robots.

Example: Implementing a Fail-Safe System in a Robot

python

CopyEdit

```python
import signal


def emergency_stop(signal, frame):
    print("Emergency Stop Activated!")
    exit(0)


signal.signal(signal.SIGINT, emergency_stop)
```

By integrating **safety-first AI principles**, we can ensure that robots are **trustworthy, responsible, and beneficial** to society.

Conclusion: Becoming a Robotics Expert

Robotics is one of the **most dynamic and rapidly evolving fields** in technology. From self-driving cars to humanoid assistants, **robots are transforming industries, workplaces, and even homes**. Becoming a **robotics expert** means continuously learning, experimenting, and adapting to the latest advancements in **artificial intelligence (AI), machine learning, automation, and sensor integration**.

This book has provided a **comprehensive foundation** in robotics, covering **robot perception, manipulation, navigation, human-robot interaction, AI integration, and debugging**. But robotics is a **lifelong journey**—to stay ahead, you must actively **develop your skills, contribute to open-source projects, and explore career opportunities**.

In this final chapter, we will explore:

✅ **How to continue learning and expanding your robotics skills.**

✅ **Open-source robotics projects and career opportunities.**

✓ **The future of autonomous robotics and your role in shaping it.**

By the end of this chapter, you will have a **clear roadmap** to becoming a successful robotics expert and making a real-world impact.

How to Continue Learning and Expanding Your Robotics Skills

1. Mastering Core Robotics Concepts

To **advance your robotics expertise**, focus on mastering these **key areas**:

Skill Area	Why It's Important
Kinematics & Motion Control	Helps design and program robot movement
Perception & Sensor Fusion	Enables robots to understand their environment
AI & Machine Learning	Powers intelligent decision-making
SLAM (Simultaneous Localization and Mapping)	Essential for autonomous navigation
ROS2 (Robot Operating System 2)	The most widely used robotics framework

Embedded Systems & IoT	Helps integrate robots with real-world applications

2. Hands-On Learning: Build and Experiment with Real Robots

Theory is important, but **real expertise comes from hands-on experience**. Build and test different types of robots:

☐ **Wheeled Robots** – Great for beginners; focus on **navigation and obstacle avoidance**.

☐ **Robotic Arms** – Learn about **inverse kinematics and precision** **control**.

☞ **Drones & Quadcopters** – Experiment with **aerial navigation** **and** **AI-based** **tracking**.

🖈 **Humanoid Robots** – Dive into **bipedal locomotion, balance, and social interaction**.

3. Setting Up a Robotics Lab at Home

To practice robotics effectively, set up a **home robotics workspace**:

✅ **Computer with ROS2 Installed** – Ubuntu is the preferred OS for ROS2 development.

✅ **Microcontrollers & SBCs** – Arduino, Raspberry Pi, or Jetson Nano.

✅ **Sensors** – LiDAR, depth cameras, IMUs, and ultrasonic sensors.

✅ **Motor Controllers** – Servo motors, DC motors, stepper motors.

✅ **3D Printer** – Useful for prototyping custom robot parts.

A well-equipped lab allows you to **test ideas, experiment with AI, and build innovative robots**.

4. Participating in Robotics Competitions

Competitions provide an **excellent way to test your skills** and network with the robotics community. Some of the top global robotics challenges include:

🏆 **RoboCup** – AI-powered soccer-playing robots.

🏆 **DARPA Grand Challenge** – Autonomous vehicles in extreme conditions.

🏆 **FIRST Robotics Competition** – Team-based high-school robotics competition.

🏆 **NASA Space Robotics Challenge** – Designing robots for planetary exploration.

By participating in competitions, you can **push your creativity, learn from peers, and gain industry recognition**.

5. Learning Advanced Robotics Topics

Once you've mastered the basics, explore **cutting-edge topics** in robotics:

🦾 **Swarm Robotics** – Multi-robot coordination inspired by nature.

☐ **Neuromorphic Computing** – AI-driven robots that mimic human brain functions.

☐ **Brain-Computer Interfaces (BCI)** – Direct control of robots via neural signals.

🌍 **Soft Robotics** – Flexible, bio-inspired robots for delicate tasks.

🖼 **Modular & Self-Assembling Robots** – Future robots that adapt their structure dynamically.

Staying updated with **emerging trends** ensures you remain at the forefront of robotics innovation.

Exploring Open-Source Robotics Projects and Career Opportunities

1. Contributing to Open-Source Robotics Projects

The **open-source robotics community** is vibrant, with thousands of developers contributing to projects that **accelerate innovation**. Some major open-source platforms include:

Project	Description
ROS2 (Robot Operating System 2)	The leading robotics framework, powering AI-driven automation.
Gazebo & Webots	High-fidelity robot simulation environments.
MoveIt!	Advanced motion planning for robotic arms.
YOLO (You Only Look Once)	Real-time AI-based object detection.
OpenCV	The go-to library for computer vision and image processing.

How to Get Started with Open-Source Robotics

✅ **Join GitHub repositories** – Find projects aligned with your interests.

✅ **Fix bugs and improve existing code** – Start with small contributions.

✅ **Develop your own ROS2 packages** – Share innovative solutions with the community.

✅ **Engage in online discussions and forums** – Learn from expert developers.

Open-source contributions help **boost your skills, build your portfolio, and connect with robotics professionals**.

2. Career Opportunities in Robotics

Robotics is one of the **fastest-growing industries**, with high demand for skilled engineers.

Career Path	Role Description
Robotics Engineer	Designs and develops robotic systems for automation.

AI & Machine Learning Engineer	Builds AI models to power autonomous robots.
Embedded Systems Engineer	Works on low-level control systems for robotic hardware.
Computer Vision Engineer	Specializes in real-time object detection and tracking.
Autonomous Vehicle Engineer	Develops self-driving cars and drones.

Industries Hiring Robotics Experts

🏭 **Manufacturing** – Industrial automation, robotic arms.

🚗 **Autonomous Vehicles** – Self-driving cars, delivery drones.

✚ **Healthcare** – AI-powered surgical robots, rehabilitation robotics.

🌍 **Agriculture** – Smart farming with AI-driven robots.

🚀 **Space Exploration** – NASA, SpaceX developing planetary robots.

How to Land a Robotics Job

✅ **Build a strong robotics portfolio** – Showcase personal projects on GitHub.

✅ **Earn robotics certifications** – ROS2, AI, and embedded systems.

✅ **Network with professionals** – Attend robotics conferences and meetups.

✅ **Apply for internships and research roles** – Gain real-world experience.

The robotics industry is **expanding rapidly**, and skilled engineers are **in high demand** worldwide.

The Future of Autonomous Robotics is in Your Hands

1. The Role of Robotics in Society

Robots will play an **increasingly significant role** in the coming decades. Some key trends shaping the future include:

AI-Powered Robotics – Fully autonomous machines making real-time decisions.

Smart Cities & Infrastructure – Robots maintaining urban systems.

Space Exploration – Autonomous rovers exploring distant planets.

Healthcare Assistance – AI-driven robotic caregivers.

As robotics experts, we have a **responsibility to develop safe, ethical, and beneficial technologies**.

2. Ethical Considerations in Robotics

With great technological advancements come **great ethical responsibilities**. We must ensure that robots:

 Respect human privacy and rights.

- **Operate within ethical and legal frameworks**.

- **Do not replace humans in ways that harm society**.

- **Are transparent and explainable in decision-making**.

Building Ethical and Trustworthy Robots

✅ **Implement strict security measures** to prevent hacking.

✅ **Develop AI models free from bias**.

✅ **Ensure human oversight in life-critical applications**.

3. Shaping the Future of Robotics

The robotics revolution is just beginning. **You** have the power to:

Design breakthrough technologies that solve real-world problems.

Develop AI-driven robots that improve lives.

- **Push the boundaries of automation** in space, healthcare, and industry.

Robotics is not just about building machines—it's about **shaping the future of humanity**.

Final Thoughts: Your Robotics Journey Starts Now!

Key Takeaways

✅ **Never stop learning**—robotics is an ever-evolving field.

✅ **Engage in open-source projects**—collaborate with the global robotics community.

✅ **Explore career opportunities**—robotics offers limitless potential.

✅ **Be ethical and responsible**—develop AI-powered robots for the greater good.

The Future of Robotics is in Your Hands!

Are you ready to build the **next generation of intelligent robots**?

Your journey as a **robotics expert** starts **now**—keep innovating, keep experimenting, and keep pushing the boundaries of what's possible!

www.ingramcontent.com/pod-product-compliance
Lightning Source LLC
LaVergne TN
LVHW051231050326
832903LV00028B/2339